HOW TO SELL ANY PRODUCTS AND SERVICES

…….. Dominating Your Market Place

Revised Edition

By:
Clinton Emscent

Acknowledgement

This piece wouldn't have been, without the beautiful ideas and knowledge of a top salesperson, whose name still rings a golden bell in the field of selling.

Dedication

Dedicated to salespeople all over the world.
I hope this piece, being an expansion of the original copy guides you as possible as it can in your selling career. Take this

as a guide in your sales arsenal. And I believe that this book will benefit you and hope you see the value of your money!
Thank you!
Happy Selling!

Table Of Contents

Fundamentals Of Selling: Sell Everything 2
How To Open Closed Doors 2
Tips On Prospecting 2
Making First Impressions Count 2
Profit By Projecting The Right Image 2
10 Ways To Boost Your Income 2
How To Help Your Prospects Make The 2
Selling Makes The World Go 'round 2
Marketing Methods 2
Open More Doors 2
The 2
Copywriting As Persuasion 2
Put More POWER In Every Sales Talk 2
Profit From A Can-do Spirit 2
Coping With Fear 2
$Power$ Closing Secrets! 2
How To Set And Reach Your Goals 2
Hunting For Prospects 2
What To Do When They Say 2
Making 2
… 8 ways to multiply yourself 2
How To Increase Mail Order Results 2
Win The Race For Success 2
The Key To Mental Fitness 2
Helpful Links 2
Selling Points To Convincing Customers 1

Selling Points To Convincing Customers

Two things have to be proven to the customer who hesitates to buy what is being offered. One is that you have the better price, and the other that you have the best available product or service suitable for his or her need.

Selling Points to use to convince customers

It is easier to use: Make comparisons. Give the customer a demonstration of how and why it is possible to save time and energy with your product.

It does the job better: Have the background knowledge to tell why your product performs more efficiently and the data with which to prove this to the customer.

More people use it: Know the statistics involved even if they refer only to the sales that you know about in actual usage.

It is dependable: Nothing infuriates the average customer more than non-performance when he is planning to use something. Experience records provide the information you need here.

Less Costly to use: Here again, experience and knowledge pays off. Have the facts at hand to convey to the customer the obvious importance of this factor and how much he can expect to save.

It will last longer: Know every detail of the guarantee and use each one on this point. Have experience of your own to present to the customer.

It is Safer: This is becoming more and more important to customers today where your item has an edge in this area… it possesses a powerful asset.

Versatility Is Superior: This is of major importance where an item does more than one thing. Usually the customer has to be shown in detail just why this is so.

It Has Prestige: This point is important. Find ways to prove it. Use the endorsements of leaders in the community or the field if you can.

It Has Exclusive Features: This point can make a big difference in the customer's decision. If there's an exclusive feature, make sure it has real value

Fundamentals Of Selling: *Sell Everything*

Selling is a profession, and as in any other profession, the people whose success are greater, are those who understands the foundation of their art. They understand that it ain't enough to just *want to sell* but also knowing *how to sell* .

The foundations are worthy to be thoroughly mastered. Don't be surprised that many sales men can not sell with the skill and ease of a real professional because they didn't and never mastered the foundations.

There are five simple fundamentals of selling, and they are;

1. *Sell yourself*
2. *Sell the company*

3. *Sell the demonstration*
4. *Sell the contract*
5. *Sell today*

All five steps are an essential part of a successful sale. Sales might be forfeited if a salesman leaves out any of this steps.

1. **Selling Yourself**

Well, your fingernails, haircut, smile, and clothes pass inspection. Your prospect is really impressed with your winning personality and the fact you bathed that day. But why should he purchase from you? What makes you so unique from other salesmen covering the same product? Well, the answer is simple-it is called *rapport*. Often begin a sale by shaking your prospect's hand, introducing your humble self with a warm, sincere smile, and placing yourself on a first name basis: *"please call me Mark" may I call you don?*

Get acquainted with the prospect and find out what interests you may have in common. It is necessary that your prospect be allowed to to identify with you and feel that you are sincere in your desire to help him meet his buying needs.

In a nutshell, you must convince your prospect that you're the right man with whom he wants to do business.

2. **Selling The Company**

Yes, the prospect is convinced that you're the right man for a business deal, but is This reason good enough for him to do business with your Company? No.

Most times, your prospect wouldn't tell you, but he really has questions about your company racing in a circle in his mind that you, must answer.

How long has your company been running? What is your company's reputation for standing behind the products they sell? How well equipped is your company for warranty? In essence, you must answer him why he Is better off doing business with your company rather than with the company "over there "

3. **Selling The Demonstration**

Product knowledge! Nothing has terminated more sales than a sales man lack of product knowledge. But who would be crazy enough?

Whether you're selling automobiles, computer, toys, pots, books, or real estate, the demonstration of your product is the base of your sale. Once, the prospect's needs has been determined, you should be able to demonstrate how your product will meet and satisfy his needs. If the prospect feels that you don't even know your own products well, the builded confidence will run down.

This, is also true, if the prospect feels that you are bly too knowledgeable about your rivals products.

4. **Selling The Contract**

Most times, a salesman begin's his sale with this step by trying to sell *price* rather than *product*, only to lose the prospect because he failed to lay the proper foundation for a sale.

If a salesman, maintains control of the sale from the start, simply by adhering to the first three fundamental steps, this should be the earliest step he discusses money with the prospect.

Most buyers are primarily concerned with how they can fit a new purchase into their budget and a salesman with a thorough knowledge of current financing options packs a potential weapon in his sales arsenal.

Never attempt to disguise costs or lead the prospect to believe he is getting more than is represented in the purchase agreement. Not only is this unethical, it is poor salesmanship. Be certain the prospect understands everything about the purchase agreement.

5. **Selling Today**

Your primary objective and goal as a salesman is to sell today, not tomorrow or the day after. Most salesmen will tell you that closing is the most difficult part of a sale.

However, professional salesmen will tell you the exact opposite is reality. Why? Because, as professionals, they understand that by following the first four fundamental steps, they have anticipated and answered most of the prospect's questions and objections, thereby turning the closing of a sale into the easiest instead of the most difficult step.

The field of sales is wide open and offers the income and professional challenge usually associated with doctors, lawyers, high-technology engineers, and corporate executives. To rise to the top of the sales profession, the medium for success is clear and easy - *sell everything*

How To Open Closed Doors

Your prospect say's he is too busy, all tied up, can't see you today. How are you going to get him to open his mind? And afterwards his door to you?

You might try one or more of these effective ways - practicalized and tested by a host of successful salesmen.

Selling is a hard tough job. To succeed, at it you must work resolution and long to do the right things. These selling ideas that work for everyother salesmen represent some of the right things.

Ask yourself this simple but worth-worthy question:
"How can i adapt,improve on,use these suggestions to get in to talk with my hard-to-see customers?"
Be on the lookout for an idea you can use in your selling today, or the first thing tomorrow morning.

1. **Be Sure To Explore All The Obvious Channels First**

Take the time to be sure that your prospect is really the hard guy to see that everyone else claims he is. The worst thing you would be doing is assuming he is, please don't. Find out, and be sure.

Try interviewing him over the telephone, or by asking his secretary for an appointment by mail if this doesn't succeed. And, of course, go to his office and ask for it, in person. Don't worry,if you're turned down,ask for an appointment still, at a time convenient for you both.

2. **Arouse His Curiosity**

The man, who is hard to be seen can be provoked into seeing you by stirring up his curiosity.

You can achieve this by simply making known your extra products or services mainly on your business card, calling card and adverts.

For instance, if you're an advertising salesman that uses highly successful ads, you can place notes saying, "i can help you plan successful ads, too."

Also a salesman selling specialist items staples miniature reproductions of his wall calendars to his business cards.

All thses are simple, easy and effective ways to use the buyer's curiosity to open closed doors.

3. **Assume That The Customer Does Have Time To See You**

Now, this is the opposite of the first rule where you don't assume that your customer is too busy to see you. Assume that your customer will talk to you he won't turn you down, if your manner of approach is right.

" Two to one, you don't get in to see him," is there a receptionist greeted a professional salesman. Our man relaxed. his mind cleared to everything but the thought of getting in to see the prospect. Finally the prospect came out. and before he could talk, the salesman stood up, briefcase in hand and ... " I am delighted to think you came out to show me into your office" he got to talk and make a sell!

4. **Make A Campaign Of It**

Make a campaign of it. Top notch salesmen label it "preheating the customer" . And you can do this through a tactiful campaign of personal calls and letters which have as their immediate objective, arousing his curiosity to the point where he wants to learn more about your product or Service.

A customer preheated is half sold. More times than not he will be anxious to hear your sales story and Grant you the appointment you need to deliver it.

A sales man in the paper products industry, see it this way "I combine personal calls with Mailings that are handled by my secretary and we watch our timing of both. In this way, I accumulate punch for each call, get to talk to the busy fellows faster, and walk out with more orders."

5. **Make It Convenient For The Customer To See You**

Be willing to see the customer or sales contact at times that are inconvenient for you to see him. But don't get into a rut. Don't think that's 9 to 5 is the best time to see your customers. the busiest ones will frequently can give you time before or after what most of us asume is the regular day.

 A case in point is that of a lumbar salesman who somewhat impatiently asked a hard-to- see contractor 'isn't their some convenient time I might see and talk to you ?" "sure" was the quick reply "come out to my home tomorrow morning and talk while I am having breakfast" now, the meeting resulted in a substantial sale. So have you ever had and 8 a.m. or 6 p.m. appointment? yes they can be had.

6. **Visit The Customer When He Least Expects To See You**

Usually this is the easiest way to talk to a hard-to-see customer. a subordinate,suggested to his boss that "this is what knowing about" produces an open door and a gladhand reception for a full sales talk.

The advantage here is that the subordinate about is usually easier to see. the effect, however, is that he might just as easily yell

"No" , the way to prevent this from happening, is to tell an incomplete sales story, concentrate on selling the subordinate on arranging the appointment. make sure that he has a complete sales story later when he has set up the interview with his superior.

7. **Take Along The Boss**

Many closed doors opens to prestige. The top brass of one company, have a lot in common with the top brass of another. And when your boss takes the time to call on a "hard to see" executive of equal or lesser rank, it is a form of flattery that the latter appreciates.

When the door opens despite the blockages, you have the opportunity to get in some hard selling.

8. Let A Mutual Friend Make The Appointment

This is an obvious approach, but frequently overlooked. Yet, it is one of the easiest ways to win an interview with a "hard to see" customer.

Salesmen, along with a great majority of the customers they call, tend to travel in similar business and social circles. Social scientists confirms this. Make the most of it, use it to your utmost advantage.

It may be fairly easy for you to find a mutual friend at the club, golf course or sales conference to introduce you to the customer you are hoping to reach.

9. Get Someone Else To Do Your Sell For You

This sales technique is slightly different from selling a subordinate or associate. Your aim here is to educate someone else concerning all the good reasons for buying your product. For example, the typewriter salesman may discreetly arrange to instruct a prospect's secretary regarding the merits of his product.

She's bound to influence her boss when he places orders for new typing equipment. The sales lesson is simple. When you can't give a personal sales talk, put the ideas into someone else's head, let him do the talking for you.

10. Shock The Customer With Showmanship

A salesman of wood-cutting machines frequently wears a shop apron over his business suit to startle 'hard to see" customers into listening to whatever he has to say. Showmanship however, need not to be far-fetched

It can be a startling statement of an important customer benefit, a dramatic display of some part of the product, or an unusual chart or diagram showing important savings, high profit potentials or other key customer benefits that result when a sale is made. The importance of what you have to say can be demonstrated, built up, dramatized by a telegram or similar communication - a call from the president of your company, a note from a "prestige" contact, a flash sales bulletin.

Keep asking yourself "how can i adapt, improve on, use these ideas to win interviews with "hard to see" customers?" Try one of these ideas on your prospects. Test them, is possible that you will end up winding up sales you never thought you would get.

Tips On Prospecting

Prospecting for sales is an essential component of the overall marketing effort. All too often new or veteran salespeople begin to think that their markets have been Saturated and that there's nowhere to go. Mastering effective prospecting techniques assures you of continued markets.

Start by identifying proper target markets. However, before you generate a list of prospects, lay out the precise market you're attempting to penetrate and why your products and services meet the needs of this market. Many salesmen and saleswomen, go "round-ringa-rose" from day to day making half-hearted attempts to penetrate first, one market, then a second and a third. They never stop to decide which market they should penetrate first -*definite of purpose* is an essential key set.

An important step in effective prospecting is to set aside time to learn about the operating characteristics of the industry. What in your past experience can be drawn upon and used as a competitive advantage in penetrating your chosen market?

What do you presently offer that is consistent with the changing needs of the target market? "Homework" mostly is an integral part of effective prospecting.

It is important to properly "work" on the prospect list that you have developed. Proper use of the list means calling all parties, using spaced intervals between calls. It also means calling everyone on the entire list and not letting the result of the first few calls dampen the enthusiasm you may have generated originally.

Develop a substantial Volume:

Many sales agents accepts to be discouraged after a relatively short time. The winners, however, realize that successful marketing means paying homage to the numbers game and, in this case,if you don't call enough numbers,it is guaranteed that you will not be a successful marketer.

It is unusual for salespeople highly depend on lists that haven't been kept uptodate or have aged. Though the temptation may be great, use only lists that you've generated yourself or, at the least, have had a hand in identifying or creating. It is discouraging to make follow-up calls on prospects who have been out or no longer active.

Effective prospecting requires the allocation of sufficient time to work the prospect list, make sales calls, follow-ups and close, and a sufficient budget in support of the sales effort. A common mistake made by salespeople is under-estimating the needed amount of time which is required to penetrate a market. Secondly, they attempt to over-economize the support of the selling effort. Thus, the adage "penny-wise and pound-foolish" makes sense here. If the best salesman in the world, needs atleast, six to seven "no's" per prospect before getting a sale, who are we then to assume that our selling efforts will require less to be successful?

You can learn something on the tenth call that is so important that it's worth calling back the first nine prospects who plainly said "No". Some other times, in working the list, information leads or new data might be generated, which will make it worthwhile to rewrite your telephone script or, in rare instances, to forego working the list for the time being.

Anticipate And Prepare For Change

One of the most essential point to acknowledge is that your target market and your efforts to penetrate it are both parts of a dynamic environment. Even the best corporate executives acknowledge that plans at times have to be altered in mid-stream. And so the saying goes "the only constant thing is change itself."

All other things being equal, the salesperson who takes the time to stay organized in working a prospect list will do far better than the one whose list isn't as such, whose notes are poorly organized, and who believes that taking 15-30 minutes a day to get organized is a waste of time.

The key to a successful personal sales effort is to offer a personal touch. Obviously, this is done best in a face to face discussion with the prospect. Many agents mistakenly believe that time can be saved by following up requests for information through the use of mail or on the phone. If you have taken the time to define an appropriate target market, develop a prospect list and work the prospect list, why take short-cuts once the prospect has been qualified by using the mail or phone rather than a personal appearance?

There's no substitute for effective prospecting. You may be a truly talented person, but if you're not making sufficient number or calls... Your compensation will agonize. Effective prospecting assures you that a healthy number of appointments can be made from which a predictable sales volume can be generated.

Making First Impressions Count

First impressions can strike you out. Or they can "the other way round". Before that potential customer standing in front of you can hear the goodness of your products or services, he has already formed his opinion of you. How? He's seen you, and depending on how successful you choose your clothes that morning, you're either on first base already or back on the dugout. In the business of business, which includes selling, "you are what you wear". Never you underestimate the power in that statement, if you do, you can strike out yourself.

To be successful you must look successful. Would you waste your time listening to sales pitch from a guy who looks unsuccessful? Of course not. You want to deal with a winner, a person who looks though he knows what he's talking about... And so does everyone else.

Plan Your Wardrobe

Gear the "Expensiveness" of your look to the price range of your merchandise. Though the business suit is standard attire for most salesmen, there are a few exceptions, as sportswear for the seller of sporting goods. Don't go overboard though and overdress, or you will risk intimidating your customers. How to find a happy medium?

More than any other garment, your suit is seen as the gauge of your ability, a symbol of authority, Blue, gray and beige are by far the most successful colors you can wear. Brown Is okay in the midwest at times but doesn't work in other areas. Stay away from black and green as they are seen as unsuccessful or even intimidating. Consider pinstriped versions f solid colors, too.

Project "Class"

Your shirt does more than hold up your necktie. Polyester-cotton blend fabric provides both good looks (resists wrinkling) and comfort. But even though most of today's shirts are "permanent press" you will improve your odds even more by having your shirts pressed. Ironing gives that fresh professional look that says you're ready for business. Knit shirts rarely cut the mustard as they don't project the well-accepted upper-middle-class look. And avoid anything shiny like the plague;

White us your most businesslike choice of shirt color. Also acceptable are light pastels, especially blue. For variation a pinstripe is okay (good choice with a solid-color suit).

Your customers judge your socio-economic status by your taste in neckties. If your necktie passes the test, people view you as reasonable-looking and respectable. The look of silk Is great, but so is it's pricetag. Polyester-silk blends and polyester ties with the look and feel of silk are less expensive and more durable. Solid-color choices might be navy, burgundy, brown, or beige - plain or with a suitable raised pattern. Tiny polkadots are fine, as are small figures such as coats-of-arms or chess pieces. Diagonally-striped patterns are classic and work well as long as they don't appear too bright or bold. Clowns belong with the circus. Proper length just touches with the belt knuckle, and a 3"- wide tie without tie tack Is presently "in style".

Coordinate Accessories

In coordinating suit, shirt and tie, practice conservatism. Unless you feel comfortable combining two patterned items, it's best to stick with one pattern and one solid. Always stay with combinations you know are winners.

Anyone knows the best clothes in the world, and won't make a poor salesman into Mr. Supersell. But what many quite talented salespeople do not seem to realize is the importance their appearance plays in getting to first base with customers. The wrong choice of outfit can mean "strike-out."

If in doubt, ask experienced salespeople how to achieve a better look. And you will find you will be approving more and more the guy looking back at you in your bedroom mirror. And so will your customers!

Profit By Projecting The Right Image

How many people you have met for the first time immediately turned you off? Unless you have been serving a life sentence in solitary confinement, your mind is now compiling a list ranked by degree of distaste. Why didn't you like them? The answers probably include such things as appearance, personality, and methods of doing business.

Most of us are fair minded folks who respect those with whom we do business. However, we also have our personal likes and dislikes. Unfortunately, we sometimes forget that everyone else has similar feelings. Being insensitive to what may displease people can be detrimental to your business.

When dealing with customers or suppliers you may unknowingly crete an unfavourable impression. A negative image also can have it's origins in the preconceived notions of the person, with whom you're doing business. The end result is the same. Two people who failed to communicate usually ends in a botched business deal.

Creating a favourable image in your business dealings may just give you an extra edge that can be translated into profits. Since your personal feelings influence your reactions to others, stop for a moment and think of the traits which you dislike. In fact, you might want to grab a pencil and make a list.

By analyzing what turns you off, you may get some insights into what is distateful to others. Modes of dress and personality quirks may arouse inborn prejudices. Someone's approach to business may annoy you. In fact, your list probably includes a wide variety of objectionable characteristics.

Plan Ahead

Reviewing your own dislikes is only the first step toward projecting a favourable image. Of equal, if not greater importance, is the examination of what might be distateful to others. Many of the things you don't like will apply universally.

Carry your evaluation further. Try to determine the likes and dislikes of anyone with whom you will be dealing on important matters during the business day. If you know anything about the individual, formulate a strategy for placing yourself in the most favourable light. Prior to any important business meeting, it's a good idea to have an informal dress rehearsal. Go over the subject matter that's scheduled for discussion. It's particularly valuable if you can get someone to act as the devil's advocate for you. They might provide to you, Constructive advice that you wouldn't think of. Anyways, you're dealing with how others see you. For this reason, an objective appraisal can be most helpful.

When in a face-to-face encounter, don't let yourself be baited by the other party. Often, leading questions will be asked in an attempt to establish your viewpoint on various topics. Sometimes others will make a deliberate attempt to rattle you. Maintain your composure. Control your emotions. Committ yourself to no controversial subject on discussions. Don't get into a debate. You can't and will not be able to change a person's long-standing opinion on an instanta. On the other hand, you shouldn't be obviously evasive, or profess ignorance of subjects that are common knowledge.

Obviously, a hostile attitude is to be avoided. At the same time, tune in on the subtleties that might come up during conversations. They could be extremely important.

Control Your Emotions

Self-confidence is indeed an important element. If you didn't have self-confidence, you won't be in business, in the first place. But, there's a fine line between showing self-confidence and projecting a know-it-all attitude. Evaluate your own personality, if you're shy, try as much as possible to rein yourself in a bit. Refrain from being pompous, or some other glitches in that manner. Track your non-verbal communication. Facial expressions, hand movements and restlessness often can create a negative impression.

However, freedom of expression Is not at issue here. You have the right to act as you choose. Of course, the party with whom you're interacting can just as readily decide not to do business with you. So to say, you don't have to force your preferences on others without being aware of the potential business consequences.

The one standard to go by in creating a proper Image is to be flexible in dealing with different situations. First impressions will always last. Whether they're favourable or not us Largely within your control.

So practice doing those things that set you apart as the right kind of person. All it has to take is time and effort n , however, it's an investment that can pay off handsomely. You will never realize whether your extra profits are due to the work you have put in on improving your image. So does that count? We all know that it's the little extras that add up to success in selling.

How To Open More Doors

Many successful salespeople gave their opinions on what they considered the essentials of an effective presentation. Many of the ideas they offered were different, but they agreed on the importance of getting their prospects involved in the presentation.

"When a buyer is allowed to sit passively and simply listen," according to one veteran salesman, "it's very difficult to one veteran salesman, "it's very difficult to overcome his natural inertia and get him to act."

You might have found this to be true in your own selling. You can, undoubtedly improve the situation dramatically by using these proven techniques for increasing your prospect's participation in your presentation. Here are some techniques that can help you reach this objective.

Does the manufacturer of your product or line of products provide a printed brochure that your customer can read? Can you finish test results?

One person who sells natural candies shows prospects a certified list of the ingredients in one of the most popular items on the line. Another offers prospects test results describing the effectiveness of a patented fuel saving device. Surveys or testimonials from satisfied customers also make excellent reading material. It is necessary to also stress any guarantee or warranty, especially if you have a copy your customers can read as you fill out the order form.

Psychologists tell us that people give a lot of weight to the written word. Use this tendency to your advantage when planning your presentation.

2. One of the best ways to gain customer involvement is to have him demonstrate the product to himself, if your item lends itself to demonstration.

3. Ask your potential customers to work out figures, using pencil and paper. Your product probably has some features that can be converted to numbers, whether it's dollars, hours saved or profit per hundred units sold. For example, suppose you sell business printing, your prospect can calculate the cost-per-item of a 1,000 form order and compare it to the cost-per-item of a 4,000 form order.

4. You can also have the prospect check your figures. "Based on a projected volume of 50 cases per week and a 45% profit margin, this new import can add some good thousands of dollars every seven days." The lend him the paper and let him check your work.

Listen And Sell

Getting started in selling can be a little scary "woohoo!" After the initial orders from Mary and Mrs Smith, the neighbor next door, realizing that you actually have to go out and call on a total stranger begins to dawn. Don't panic! I'm about to give you a sure-fire cure for the cold call heebie-jeebies.

Nothing makes us appreciate friends and relatives more than spending a few days pounding on very cold doors. You will discover that one of the main reasons your friends bought was because they like you!

Go ahead and ask "how can I make friends… people who will buy from me?" The answer is ridiculously simple…. By listening to them!

Listen to what they have to say when you're going to pitch or make your sales. A prospective customer might start telling you about their last summer trip, listen, smile and allow them to finish their tale, especially when they are telling you about something more "in-person" like their family, friends or even pet. When you listen to them, and be active with them, you have automatically become a friend or even a family friend and surely they will repay you back for your time by making an order!

Questions Open Doors

You can watch this listening technique first hand by visiting a new car showroom. Successful auto salesmen will talk very little - if at all, about their product. Their presentation consists of asking a number of pertinent questions such as "will your wife (husband) be driving it too? Are you planning to use the car for long vacation trips or just around town? What's your favorite color? Do you have children who may be drivers?

Each question will give the prospective customer a chance to relate a story and each story told will draw him closer to the listening salesman. After a while, he becomes a friend... not just a salesman.

Still unconvinced? Drive out to a small town and stop at a gas station. Put a bewildered look on your face and ask the attendant for directions to pleasantville. I guarantee that not only will you receive directions from the fellow at the pump but also from the station manager, the little old lady who is walking by and the druggist Next door. All of these people want to help *because you want to listen.*

Would you believe some people actually get paid for listening? They're called psychiatrists, and they make real good money.

Your customer's stories, points-of- view and tales are very much Important because they enable him to become the main performer and center of attention. Keep in mind that other people (his wife, children, secretary or co-workers) probably are too busy to take time off and be good listeners. Think of the pleasure he can derive from your visit... if you will listen attentively. And think, too, of the large order that you're likely to get as a reward for being attentive.

10 Ways To Boost Your Income

Faith is the essential ingredient in every success. One must believe that the job can be done and that he can do it. The reality of the vision assures one that ultimately he will reach his goal. Some of the basic success factors include:

1. Believe In Yourself: the little engine that was determined to climb the mountain kept assuring itself ," I think I can, I think I can" and with that resolve and determination, it laboriously climbed the mountain, scaled through the highest peak and then joyfully sang out as it rolled down the mountain, "I thought I could, I thought I could." It was the little engine's belief in itself that enabled it to reach its goal!

The salesman, too, must have the resolve to achieve. Self-assurance puts the salesman ahead so that he can do the job and meet whatever situation he encounters.

2. *Believe in your Product:* The salesman must be sold on his product if he is to sell it successfully. The prospect can detect the salesman's insincerity or lack of knowledge by observing the way he deals with questions. One can't talk convincingly about his product unless he knows a lot about it.

☐**3. *Believe In Your Company:*** Are you sold on your company's methods of operation? You should believe that it is the best in it's field. Is it consumer oriented?

If your company enjoys a good reputation, you have an advantage. Be proud that you are in an important part of such an organization.

4. Believe In Your Customer: By and large your customer is practical, down-to-earth and knows what he wants. Don't discount his sincerity nor undervalue his knowledge. Believe in your customer's sincere desire to buy your merchandise. Assure yourself that he is ready and willing to buy.

5. ***Believe In The Strength Of Sincerity:*** It is one of the most important elements of successful selling. Sincerity demands that the salesman do his best to properly handle the Interview, to answer questions and to furnish the important details which the customer should know. It requires the salesman to do his best to please the customer, to give him good service, to make him happy with his purchase. Sincerity can mean real dollars in additional sales.

6. Believe In The Effectiveness Of Your Demonstration: Be sure you have devised a demonstration that will most effectively show your merchandise and answer questions which the prospect may have. The demonstration sells or unsells the merchandise.

7. Believe In Frankness: So much more for the rule in Number 5. If you do not know the answer to a question, don't pretend you do. It may get you into serious trouble. Tell the prospect frankly that you do not know but will get the information… and make sure that you really do. So much for building relationships? You bet.

If the customer is called away and then returns, be positive he recalls what happened. Don't bore him with a lot of details which he knows but be sure he gets all the facts. Take up where you Left off and continue smoothly. Remember, the sale may he riding on the effectiveness of the demonstration.

8. Believe in Systematic Organization: Keep your working materials in tiptop shape so that the interview will be smooth, pleasant, friendly and timesaving.

Don't take an unusual amount of time for the interview unless the customer is relaxed, unhurried and in the mood to buy.

9. Believe In Keeping In Touch With Your Customers: Competitive salesmen are bidding for business, making special offers to induce them to buy. Your customer is a busy man with a hundred and one things to divert his mind from you and your merchandise.

Customers are like flowers. They need constant attention and care. They should think of you often and be aware of what you can do for them.

There are many things the salesman can do to assure that he is remembered. Use the phone frequently. It is handy, saves time and is a money maker. If a prospect had told you about his daughter on the varsity team, inquire about her progress. If he usually talks about anything outside business, indulge him lightly. If he doesn't, stick to business.

10. Believe In Your Own Success: The man who succeeds Is the man who believes he can. Feel that you are going to succeed. Like the little engine, believe that you have the power and the rugged determination to scale the mountain and you will meet and beat any "Gigantic Mountain".

Be a problem solver

Successful selling and problem solving go hand-in-hand. Learn all you can about your prospect's problems. See what they need. That's the essence of Successful selling.

If you can solve problems, you can close sales. It's as simple as that.

How To Help Your Prospects Make The "Right" Decisions

How come we don't sell every prospect we talk to?

Well, there's this reason and that reason, no money and no need. But it we sit down and examine our presentation thoroughly, more often than not we'll find a common explanation of why we didn't make the sale. We just didn't ask for the order.

You may think that you're going through the closing process, but the prospect may not recognize the fact that you are trying to ask for an order. Basically, the act of closing is simply making decisions with

which the prospect will agree. You might ask, for example, any of the following questions:
"You like this color, don't you?"
If you get a "yes," you've made a sale, even though they don't say "wrap it up" "isn't this the best spot for the panels?"
Again, a "yes" means it's sold- and they don't have to say "can you start tomorrow?"

Build Good Closing Questions

Consider that a good closing Question is one in which the answer you get indicates the prospect has brought. Remember, too, that the customer often won't be all that specific about making the purchase. We often have to assume they want to buy, even though they may not say so.

Why don't salespeople close all the time? Why don't we always ask for the sale? The chief reason is *fear*. We don't like to be rejected. While it may be hard to remember, you aren't being rejected personally if you don't get the order. They just aren't buying your product. It has nothing to do with you.

Besides, what are they gonna do that's so terrible? Slam the door in your face? Curse you? No, of course not! They're going to say, "we just aren't in for it. Can't afford it now. Thanks for letting us know about it, we'll see you again next month." That's not too terrible, is it? When we consider the worst that can (the word "no"), getting turned down isn't all that bad. So, let's ask for the order each time.

How can we do that? Well, there are two types of closes we can use... the direct and the indirect.

The direct is just that... "Do you want to buy this?" Although it's blunt, the message is there. And since you are asking for the sale, you will get your share. Many salesmen prefer the indirect approach which has three methods.

The first is the assumptive close. You assume they are going to buy your products. All the way through, you assume they will buy. If you do a good job, they will.

The second is one many salesmen use. Offer an alternate. "Would you prefer to start here, or would over there be better?" When they say "where?" They have bought. It's an either-or proposition here. They aren't asked "yes" or "no."

The "Suggestion" Approach

The third indirect method Is the suggestion approach. "It appears to me that this would be the best spot for the cooling unit, don't you think?" A "yes" and you've sold it, too!

Pick out the best closing method for you and use it.

But there's more to closing than just asking for the order. The closing process runs all through the sales presentation itself... from the start to finish. The better we understand that, the more sales we'll make.

Naturally, we always want to qualify prospects before we even talk to them... make sure they need our product and can afford it. Second best is to be sure and qualify them when you start your presentation. That way they can't throw the "no money" or the "no need" objection at you when you tell them the price.

Try to condition the people to expect a close as you talk with them. All through your presentation, try to build the value of what you're selling so the price will seem small by comparison. Remarks like "this is one heck of a good investment" can do the trick.

Use Props

You can use physical means to promote the sale. Hand the prospect the contract. Hand him a pen. Then the burden of saying "no" is on him. You've indirectly asked for the sale just by your actions.

Throughout the presentation, provide reassurance to your product. After all, it he buys your product, he'll have to defend his decision to others. People will say, "what, you bought the LLL skincare products!" Give him reasons to defend himself and his decision. We all have to explain to others (friends, relatives, etc.) Why we did that, why we bought from them and so on. The more ammunition we can provide for our customers, the better off we are. People think of this problem as you talk to them. They are asking themselves, "Gosh, how'll I explain that to Linda?" *Help them.*

The final step in interweaving the close through your presentation is to talk in pictures. Help the prospect see the benefits your product will provide. You can do this with literature, testimonial letters and so forth. Put your man in the picture.

Now that you know you must ask for the sale and understand how to weave the close into your pitch, perhaps you're still worried about closing. Here's a sure-fire method for you, one that will close nine out of ten prospects.

Look directly at your prospect. Say, in your own words, something like this, "we've talked a lot today, covered a lot of ground, our prouducts, how it works, what to expect, and all that, I've been so very thorough with you because I have been anxious to help make an intelligent decision." With this format, it doesn't matter if you're speaking in person or over the phone, or "text" as the case may be. But in today's selling, most of the transacts are done with and through digitally. In anyway, just do your job well in the presentation, and yes, after all is said, it's up to the prospect to make the right decision!

Selling Makes The World Go 'round

No matter what you do or how you do it, in the end you have to he a salesman... a good salesman... to be a real success.

Many people call themselves secretaries, carpenters, plumbers, seamstresses or electricians. They may consider themselves lawyers, teachers, accountants or psychologists. But, strip away these superficial labels that describe their skills and, in the end, you'll find that they're selling all the time... it they're any good at their work.

Okay! you ask, what is selling? *It's pleasing someone do that they respect your product or service and decide to buy it."*

When that happens you're a salesman and you've made a sale. It's that simple.

People who begin to think of themselves as salespersons, no matter what they do, have taken the first step toward success in their work!

A Top-Notch Salesman

A top-notch salesman is one who makes sure his work isn't "satisfactory" but "exceptional" who is willing to put in extra effort and time to deliver. Just sell your skill, your capability and enthusiasm on every job you got to tackle.

How To Build A Business

Permit me to tell you the story of a craftsman-salesman. Once, a client of his was curious as to how much work he was doing whether he had many requests to sand floors, work for which he advertised. When this was inquired of him, he said requests for his services were rather erratic, sometimes big, sometimes small, but it really didn't matter to him. He explained that he, his wife and his son had another interest. This "other" Interest made the most of his trade skills and assured a steady income for his family, and kept him busy.

Mark and his wife periodically look at homes which are advertised for sale. When they find one that is under-priced or low-cost, because it has problems, particularly the kitchen and bathroom, they buy it. After doing this, they sell their current home, and move in to the one they just bought.

Between sanding jobs and on weekends, the family remodels their new home, He had learned that the kitchen and bathroom were the two most important rooms for every "home searchers". By fixing up the kitchen and bathroom, well equipped too, and house well painted and fixed up, he then sell it at a much higher price than before. And the hustle continues over again.

A Positive Attitude

Would you say that mark is a home remodeler or a salesman? He probably is an "extinct" breed of craftsman-salesman, but I would hope not. The world needs more people like him. Perhaps, most of all, it needs the kind of salesmanship that he achieves through quality work. When mark began to think of himself as a salesman, he took the first step toward the success that he now enjoys.

Two types of people are working for a living today, salespeople and non-salespeople. A salesperson is a man or woman who is on the ball, who works in a way that is bound to please others. The more salespeople a company has and the fewer non-salespeople, the more likely it is to be profitable and to grow.

Many people engaged in direct selling are in business for themselves. Others work for companies upon which they are dependent for recognition and pay. Whether we call on prospects or hold other jobs with other duties, we must avoid getting into a rut when we think of our responsibilities and our abilities to carry them out. No matter what we do, we can and should think of ourselves as salespeople. Viewing our work on this light will give us a better insight into other people. It also will improve our relationships with the suppliers whose products we handle.

Put The Customer First

When we go to work each day, we should think about our customers and their needs. We should ask ourselves how people can benefit through our efforts, how we can serve them better by doing our jobs more effectively. *We should think about people like mark and try to be as conscientious about our work as he is.*

It takes salespeople in every department of an Organization today to make a company grow and prosper, not just those who make sales calls. Whether you are out on the road as a salespeople or not, start doing things to please people. It will make your work more pleasurable, give you more satisfaction and add to your income. *People who think of themselves as salespeople, no matter what their jobs, are bound to succeed.*

Marketing Methods

Sales Experts Agree that to succeed in selling you've got to be Salesminded! They mean that you should be thinking about your job and doing something about promoting sales every possible minute.

Planning is part of the thinking you must do. Generally speaking, planned presentations are the best presentations. They prepare too to answer questions that customers are likely to ask. Planning also enables you to be prepared to vary your approach as circumstances dictate.

Selling starts with your thinking about it. If you think positively and are optimistic, you are on the right track. Your appearance must coincide with what you say.

if you aren't truly salesminded, the right kind of training can do the job for you. Here is what you should do:

- Learn all you can about your prouduct or service. Never feel that you already know all there is to know. You will find that you'll uncover something new as well as something that you've forgotten. Furthermore, there's another benefit that you can get from studying and reviewing what you're selling. Pick out something special or unique and use it in your next sales presentation. Look for features that you can promote, ideas that may be especially important to specific prospects. Keep looking for factors such as value, conversation of energy, greater productivity, ease of maintenance, simplicity of operation and others. You are sire to find features that will help you do your job more effectively!

- The needs of prospective customers deserve your constant attention. How well do you know those needs? Where can you get that information? Will these people be easy to sell? If you were planning a job interview you would make an effort to know as much as possible about the company beforehand. You would also be prepared to talk about your potential contributions. Think and act the same way before each sales presentation. It's the best sales technique around.
- Consider your regular customer's needs. Start by reviewing your records. Have you kept up with changes in their programs? Do you have the latest information about their prouducts or the equipment they use? Is it possible that they need new products or services that you can provide? If you have been missing the

boat with these customers, you still have time to catch up.

- You must get and maintain the tools that salespeople need. Don't confuse these tools with those used by carpenters and mechanics. A salesperson's tools are his education and training, his skill at approaching customers, his use of language, his sales literature and samples and his helpful attitude. Keep these tools sharp.
- If you're truly salesminded, check up on how you greet people, the expressions You use and the way you handle yourself. Decide whether you talk too much or too little. Do you always offer to help people with their problems or only when you think it will lead to a sale? Are you always friendly? How do you react when your request for an order is turned down? These mannerisms

are very important because people who respect and trust a salesperson are more easily persuaded to buy from him or her.
- Have you set sales goals? You aren't really salesminded unless you have. Review what your customers have been buying and look for ways to get them to increase their orders by five or ten percent. Check yo see if these customers are buying your best model, the largest size or the latest style. A few appropriate words may tip the scales to a larger dollar order. If any of your customers are expanding their operations, you may be able to set your sights at a 20 to 25 percent order increase.
- Being motivated to sell means that you always are looking for new customers. But have you thought about where you are most likely to find

them? Spend some time thinking about it. Discuss the problem with your friends and relatives. Just one suggestion may pay off!
- Dedicated salespeople never forget the customers they used to have, those that stopped buying for one reason or another. Go over your records to see what they were buying and then call on them. Perhaps prices have changed or, possibly they are dissatisfied with your competition. They may have new needs but simply haven't called on you. You have nothing to lose and much to gain by renewing old acquaintances.
- Now, do you agree that you have got to be salesminded to be successful? More important, have you been thinking about the things that really count? If you are like most salespeople you haven't spent a great

deal of time on the techniques and strategies of selling. But, it's never too late . Get salesminded and watch your sales increase.

Open More Doors

The human "ego" can set some awful traps for people, especially for direct salesmen. It is essential that we understand the fact that people take pride in their work and their achievements. If we provide recognition, reflecting honesty and sincerity in the manner in which it is done, it's likely that our prospects will have a higher regard for us.

Make Favourable Comments
Look for little things that merit comment. For example, the buyer has modernized his shop or office. Notice the improvements with a comment such as, "you certainly have done a great job in furnishing your place. I enjoy coming here because it's so attractive." Your favourable comment can go a long way

toward building a better relationship with the prospect.

Another way of complimenting your prospect is to remark on a suit or tie he may be wearing. "Where do you buy your clothes, Mr Pulte?" Provides an implied compliment and an opportunity for a brief discussion… with a chance for him to offer advice on where to get good items.

Such an approach will probably inflate your prospect's ego. You accomplish two things by your approach. First, you recognize the prospect's good taste and, second, you give him a chance to be helpful to you. Most people like to feel that they are useful to others. They enjoy a chance to be "experts." Subconsciously, they enjoy an invitation to lend a hand if they can do so without inconvenience or expense.

It's human nature to enjoy opportunities for approval and acceptance by others. The wise salesperson provides these opportunities wherever it is possible to do so. We all need to have our morale bolstered from time to time. Let's not neglect opportunities to provide such an elixir.

"Timing," it often has been said, "is the essence in decision-making." It also is the essence in opening a sales presentation. If you are to be successful in closing sales, you must first be competent in opening them. One is as important as the other, and neither is complete in itself.

Avoid Interruptions

Try to time your opening remarks at the most opportune time… certainly not when your customer is preoccupied with customers or wok. To interrupt a prospect when he or she is preoccupied with another person is rude. It can close the door to a presentation. Yet, I have seen salespeople interrupt prospects because they were in a hurry to get to the next account as quickly as possible.

Put bluntly, this is nothing less than selfishness. Naturally, salespeople want to make as many calls as possible. At the same time, they have to show proper respect for those who are giving them time to talk to them. That tired old phrase "haste makes waste" can be applied to situations of this nature.

Although many salespeople don't realize it, by working slower you actually may be working more efficiently.

Arouse Curiosity

The point *I*'m trying to make is that by arousing curiosity, suspense or interest, you often will get your prospect to talk first. He has no time to dwell on negative thoughts such as, "I have more of those than I need" or "Come back some other time when I have more money available."

Such remarks are equivalent to saying "no." They are euphemisms for closing the door.

There was salespeople who were, in the strictest sense, actors. They know every nuance of the trade. And merchants waited for their arrival… just to be entertained and "sold." There is something in human nature that says, "Show me! Entertain me and earn the orders that I place with you."

Give your customers what they want. All it costs is your time. If he or she wants to be entertained, be certain that you do it well... but always keep an eye on the "close"

Give your customers your undivided attention, as you would your companion when out on a date, As a general rule, good listeners sell more. And show your customers that you appreciate their patronage. Thank them in person or hy letter if necessary.

Your attitude toward others shows not our in your speech but also through your actions. We can't successfully hide our feelings behind a wall of smiles and small smiles. So show your genuine concern for others. If you do, more doors, for sure, will be opened to you and your order lists will be the envy of your colleagues.

BE PREPARED To leave customers with something to remember you by, such as a sample or a brochure. You can return later to ask the prospect how he liked the product or to pick up the literature. And you may pick up an order, as well. This tactic is especially effective with customers who are too busy to talk or who don't think they're "in the market right away"

DIRECT SELLING Often has been called "the nursery of free enterprise." When new products are being tested, they frequently are exposed to the public for the first time through direct selling. That's why you and other direct salespeople often do so well and make so much money. You benefit from virgin markets.

You'll find new marketing ideas In direct selling and a host of new products year after year. Keep abreast. Learn all you can about the companies and the plans they are offering. One good merchandising plan can put you on top!

SAFETY for the home and business has grown into a giant among industries. People are always looking for the best ways to protect themselves and their possessions. Protective devices that notify the cops of an invader In a dwelling or place of business are available. You can choose the model you feel you can work with. Then, get out there and begin making profits through big commissions.

REMEMBER that every day Is a new day. Wipe the slate clean. If yesterday didn't go well, don't let it influence your behavior. Begin fresh and profit from the experiences you have had. As one writer put it, "Success comes to those who know it isn't coming and go out and get it."

Optimism is essential in selling. Believe that you're the best and what you're selling is the best. Customers pick up on that feeling!

The "Magic Factor" In Selling

Looking for a model of good salesmanship - one that will stick and be a constant reminder of how to do a lot of things right? Don't look any further! Look at that admirable and time-honored stage performer, the veteran magician.

Yes, the accomplished "magic man" is unique, because he does so many things that are right. And by the way, in setting him up as an example, we are obviously referring to his showmanship and not to the tricks he uses to deceive an audience.

Anyways, let's look at several of the magician's plus points and how they apply to better salesmanship.

First, *the magician is prepared*! That's a real plus! The man of magic knows his ground, because he has checked over the stage, lighting, seating capacity and all his props. He has practiced all his tricks with an eye to showing them in the best style possible. By show time, he's confident - and ready.

Once the performance starts, there is no doubt as to who is directing things. The magician makes things happen, thanks to his careful planning and his positive thinking about how well he will be received. He holds the audience breathless at times, as they wait for his next act because he is absolutely in command.

Second, ***the Magician is a showman.*** Deftness is the master of the day, as the magician gestures in perfect syncing with his verbal descriptions. When he says, "Now you're going to see..." everybody strains to see. As he taps his magic wand against a silk hat or verse, necks are stretched in the audience so that nothing will be missed. It's creative, planned showmanship all the way... and the audience loves it.

Third, ***the magician... demonstrates!*** The visual element is very much a factor in the magic business, as it should be in selling. Showing something, demonstrating, giving the crowd something to watch is a part of the stage magician's act. It adds that extra dimension to his performance. He knows he will be most effective if his spoken words are only a supplement to a lot of things happening visually.

Fourth, ***The magician gets others into the act!*** This is important in the magic business, and in selling. What, after all, is even more effective than a vivid demonstration? Here's the answer: *placing the products in the customer's hands!*

Obviously, depending on your product, this isn't always possible. But whenever you can let that customer feel, touch, taste , hear , or heft the thing you're selling, you will have the person more than half sold. It's one of the oldest selling fundamentals - *involvement leads to action.*

And right here stop and think. Isn't the magic show suddenly more personally interesting to you when the performer, showing mastery of his stagecraft, pulls someone from the audience to help? You bet! In doing so, the magician has suddenly made more of a show of it.

Fifth, **the magician closes the sale.** There's a conclusion to every act the magician performs. Creatively, he catches your interest, then builds your desire to see him finalize his act. With supreme showmanship, he demonstrates (with high visibility) ... and then, he closes his sale! He finalizes in a way that brings smiles of satisfaction to all.

As you sell creatively, it might be good to remember the methods of creative salesmanship, the able magician! He *Sells!* And we can all learn a lesson from him.

Copywriting As Persuasion

We will go simple, straight and to the bone on this.

Selling itself is persuasion, it should be, in its nature. But funny enough, not every salesperson is actually *persuading*. Now ask yourself *"are you persuading Your prospects?"* Yes or no? If you're not trying to persuade, then you're not trying to sell! As simple as that.

Persuasion is a deliberate attempt to enact change. So when you are trying to sell, you're deliberately trying to make a decision for your prospect, one they won't, and can't resist. It actively involves a **Sender** (you as the salesperson), **A receiver (** Your prospect) **and A Feedback** (from your prospect).

Always keep it in mind that *Emotion drives Action, and information drives analysis.* You should always try to bring up an emotional slide in your sales presentation. When they *feel* an *emotion,* they are going to take action, and the information needed is the one you are going to provide, the sweetness, the benefits etc, is left for them to check if they really do want it, or at least if it's true? Which can be achieved by providing customer's positive reviews!

Four Facts About Every Reader

.1. **They** are not idiots

2 They are under no compulsion to read what you have written, still less to keep reading it, once they have started.

3 They have other things to do

4 They have other things that matter to them!

…. So, you're going to make it important to them!

Now, we have formulas in copywriting, and we are going to have a look at the basic and general Two.

AIDA:
A= Attention
I= Interest
D= Desire
A = Action

The point is, your sales copy should follow this route and formula. It should be able to get people's attention, spark up their interest, bring in Desire to have that (Emotion comes into play) and then drive them to take Action. We will talk more on this later.

Using TIPS in Copywriting
TIPS
Where **T= Tempt**

I = Influence: Entertain your prospects first, deliver the satisfaction you promised when you tempted them. Then start working on their deeper motivations.

P= Persuade: The evidence, the special offers, the testimonials, the money-back guarantee, and all the sweetnesses.

S= Sell: Use the four R's which are "Repeat your story", "Remind them of the main benefits", "Reassure them that they are making the right decision", and "Relieve them of their money".

Writing Irresistible Headlines

Remember, you have to get your prospects' attention first, and to do that, you need an irresistible Headline in writing your sales copy.

Features tell, Benefit sells. The difference between features and benefits is that features make the show, while Benefits wins the show. Not that features aren't needed, but your prospect is much more interested in the benefits.

The best Headlines convey 2-3 benefits.

Headline Type: List Headlines
Example: 3 ways to…
3 steps to…
The 7 best …
The top 10…
Take these 3 simple steps to clear your face acne and get rid of pimples quickly

People most times love to go through steps, and that is the effectiveness of this type of headline. You're using steps and people are more likely to get through steps or, and instructions. Make sure to always put power into your headlines.

Headline Type: How To Headlines

How to do…
How to be…
How to make…
How to do x without x
How to have x without x

In "How To" headlines, (and even others) you should always add something real, don't add vague words, don't make it boring, make it realistic and if possible, (when would they reach their goal?"

Also note that adding "Numbers" or "lists" can add more effect.

Example:

How to have acne-free skin without acne creams in 7 days!

How to grow your hair without oils in a week!

How to be a homeowner in 5 days

Etc … the list goes on…

Headline Type: High click-through headlines
You won't believe…
Incredible story of…
Isn't this awesome…
Fake but true…

Evoke emotion on all your headlines, Remember you're giving them a reason to click, or to compel or to read.

Remember, always add power words, yes say Clickbait? If your headline doesn't evoke curiosity or strike any force, forget it.

Headline Type: Questions Headlines
Are you?...
Do you?...
Is there?...
Have you?...
Is it?...

Use question headlines to strike high clicks.

Writing Content That Sells

In writing content that sells, there are a few basic rules we must adhere to.

In writing sales content, which is sales post, some basic rules should come into play. Before we move on, note that not all contents you write should be selling something. This applies mostly if you have a website or Blog for your business. It is also applicable on, for example, on your social media page. You shouldn't always make sales posts, right?

Do not make your paragraph too long. 2-3 sentences is okay. Your aim is to enact change and influence the prospect's action, and believe it or not, you are going to do that with as short but persuasive and sweet words as possible.
There should always be consistency, that is, a relation between the headline and the text.
Write for everyone. Don't and stop using long words and big words. Write for the common man. Write as simply as possible.
The longer the content, the more images needed.
Now, with our formula AIDA , all of your Contents Should follow this formula.
Title Should get the Attention
Title and first paragraph Should bring in the Interest

Third and fourth paragraph Should bring the Desire
And the fourth or last paragraph brings in the Action.

Put More POWER In Every Sales Talk

Examine Potential Problems

Quick question; what is the problem of selling? The question is an ever timely one for every salesmaker. Resultful and profitable problem solving activities are an indispensable ingredient of successful salesmanship.

Made more specific, this question might be: What is the central problem that is basic to every selling situation? Is it making calls to service customers or to find prospects? Is it selling more of your company's products and services? Is it pioneering the establishment of new markets? Or is it maintaining a good company image? Or is it none of these? (Hmmm).

There's something that comes naturally to most thoughtful

salemakers. What is it? Selling your ideas and concepts. Most central problems, basic to every situation, need persuasion. Now, to the main point, **Motivation**.

A great and accomplished business man once said *"The basic function of all marketing activities aimed at developing sales is not to sell but to motivate customers and prospects to want to do business with us. The end result of all our sales promotion and market development activities, if we do a good job of using our selling tools are capabilities, is more sales, more business, more profits, more customers buying your goods and services. The central problem of selling is therefore, how to persuade, inspire, and motivate our customers and sales prospects to do business with us rather than with the competition."*

Identify Objectives

And, so it is in selling: motivation is the central, over-riding concern of the salesmaker. There are three simple things every salesmaker must learn to do well - ***Set call objectives, sell benefits, and ask for the order.***

Let's take call objectives. After a salesman makes a call, the sales manager will ask him what was the objective of the call. The man invariably answers that he called on the sales contact to introduce a new product or that he wanted to explain a new service his company is offering... This is not a call objective because it was stated in terms of what the salesmaker intended to do. A means by which he was trying to achieve an objective. The objective must be stated in terms of some action to be taken by the prospect or customer.``

This advice is excellent. Every problem is part of a bigger problem. And the problem in all selling is what do you do about the problem once you have identified it? What constructive steps do you take to find a solution to the problem that results in a profitable exchange between you and the sales contact?

What To Do

Identifying a problem and successfully resolving it is a day-in-day-out concern of the best of salesmakers… and it involves six presentation steps in this order of priority:

A Theme; Every worthwhile sales presentation contains a short, clear, and memorable statement of the selling proposition: "This is what's in it for you, Mr Rightman!"

A Promise Of Gain; Every Sales Talk includes an equally clear and specific statement of how the listener will profit from some new action taken with respect to your suggestions or offerings: "Specifically, these are the several ways you will benefit, Mr Rightman!"

A Problem; Every sales talk addresses itself to a customer problem. It's accurate identification is of paramount importance to the success of the entire talk.

A Solution; Every Sales talk contains a highly believable solution that will fulfill the promise of gain made earlier in the talk.

Proof; Every good sales presentation uses facts, case histories, and success stories to document the desirability and certain success of the recommended solution.

Action; Every productive sales presentation contains a motivator. This, finally, is the central objective of every selling effort! The customer must be motivated, he must react, he must agree to move in some positive manner. Only then does he put his name on the order form or approve your suggestions with a welcome "I'll buy it!"

Next time you make a call, ask yourself, "what's the problem?" Make sure you have the right answer. Then sell with solutions that motivate the customer to buy!

Touch And Sell

There's a proven, easy way for salespeople to increase their sales immediately. It's free, relaxing and enjoyable. It's called a gentle touch.

Scientists now know that touching causes immediate relaxation in the person touched. By eliminating tension, touching allows a feeling of trust to develop.

Gentle touching involves more than a handshake, although that's a good start. The best place to touch a customer is on the hand, wrist or upper arm. These places signal your friendliness. Don't resort to slaps on the back, thinking more is better.

Remember, these are gentle touches. One of two touches during your sales pitch are more than enough. Don't be obvious about it. The customer should not be conscious of your gentle touch. It should come naturally. But subconsciously, it's likely that he or she will respond with positive feelings towards you and what you're selling. And that can make the difference between a customer who walks and one who buys!

Ask For The Order

"ONe of the big problems facing business today is that salesmen have forgotten how to sell." Said the keynote speaker at a sales seminar.

He made another hard-hitting point by asking, "when's the last time a home appliance salesman called you at home and asked if he might bring a new model for a test.?"

That lack of salesmanship abounds in every line of business. Now, how many direct sales people check back on old customers to see if they're ready to re-order or to show them new products that their suppliers are featuring? How often do you do this yourself?

Those who wish to succeed must go out after sales. Success in selling depends on how many times you ask for an order. It takes a lot of shoe leather. Persistence is more important than any other consideration. It's more important than a college education. Remember, there are a lot of educated failures.

Profit From A Can-do Spirit

Wouldn't it be a tremendous lift and benefit to you if you could maintain an "up" and "can-do" optimistic attitude every day of your selling career? Goals, eventually, would be reached, impossible problems would be solved, and your achievements could exceed your wildest dreams... if only you could keep a winning spirit regardless of the situations or circumstances that arise.

Well, there's a way to have a bright outlook every day, and that's what we'll talk about here. A realistic, optimistic, *"can-do"* spirit is the key to your success in selling anything! It is the key to your growth and professional development.

Here's a recommendation on how to do it: Start each day by setting your specific objectives for the day. Vow to yourself to maintain your output and build your proficiency. If you see the moves you're making beforehand, and if you generally like the direction in which you're moving, it's much easier to maintain a positive attitude. In other words, if you know how to play a game, and you feel it's possible to win, it's fun!

Avoid Negative Thoughts

You might find it helpful to realize that negative thoughts, worry and despair are all perfect examples of negative creative thinking. Often, negative, self-destructive thinking comes from concentrating too heavily on nitpicking irritants and worrying too much about mistakes in the past or possible mistakes in the future…

Instead of making the very best of the moment and the day you have in hand.

Believe me, if you develop the bad habit of focusing on the worrisome and dismal, you become proficient at it. You can make your life and your daily activities an absolute chaos.

Jealousy or envy, for example, are particularly destructive. The classic silent statement that wells up within you when jealousy grabs you is: "why does he or she have so much good fortune? I'm just as skillful as he or she is. Why don't I receive money, adulation, and praise he or she gets?".

Here's another example of self-destructive thinking: "I don't like my selling job! I got this position by mistake. For one thing, I don't like working with people, and that's what I'm forced to do."

And how about this one: "why should I have to do the dirty work? Why is it necessary for me to work my way up when the boss's son moved right into a top spot?"

Put Your Prospect First

All of these grievances, whether expressed outwardly or felt inwardly, lead to one result: The people you contact feel something is amiss or radically wrong in you. Your negative spirit and attitude are deadly… and people in a very simple but final way. They don't buy from you. Why? Because you're communicating that you are thinking more about yourself than you are about their needs and wants.

To prevent such a losing situation, make sure your attitude is right. Think straight, accurately and positively! Realize that the name of your game is to serve people... with integrity and Professionalism. You do it with whatever knowledge and skills you now have or are developing. Doing so will help you release greater energy and enthusiasm.

There may have been a time in history when you could get away without continuous growth and development, but not anymore. Today, in our fast-moving world, you have to keep reaching, stretching and improving your performance all of your life. To get ahead and stay there, you must develop the habit of constantly sharpening your skills.

How about your future goals? Are they realistic? Have you set them with an open, hopeful, outgoing attitude? Are they really what you want? Are they high enough? Do you have an exciting, believable plan to reach your goals?

You need to think positively, hopefully, as you stretch your thinking as to how to reach these objectives. Meditate on each goal and on your comprehensive plan to reach it and don't be afraid to burn the midnight oil. Put your plan on paper, sketching in all details. Make sure your plan is set.

Project A "Positive" Image

Day after day, put down all the positive actions you can take to reach your goal. This very act can work wonders for you. There's something about getting a pen in hand and writing down what's on your mind. As the french say, " The appetite comes with the eating!" Creative thoughts come when you start to create… and your pen and paper can be the catalyst.

Set attitude improvement goals by saying, "I'll develop a more positive attitude, an "up" feeling in all of my daily activities. I'll look for and mark the tremendous possibilities for growth and I'll capitalize on these possibilities. I'll keep a record of all my plans so that none will slip away."

Can you think of other ways to develop a more positive mental set? If you can, why not write them down right now? You can say, "I'll develop a "can do" attitude toward those I serve. I'll get a jump on each situation by asking crisp, well-phrased questions… and I'll decide on plans of action based on meeting the needs of my clients."

Visualize yourself performing as an extremely successful professional. Find ways to top your present performance. You might say, "my model to emulate is this person. She solves problems this way. She finds people's needs and wants that way… and then she pours in the multiple, excellent benefits of his products and services.

Establish Goals

"Now, I won't copy. You will see my fingerprints, my personality, on what I do. However, this image of excellence has afforded me valuable clues which I'll now try to put into practice. Every day I will keep refining, honing and correcting... until I get my daily procedures just the way I want them. And, this learning and growing can continue throughout my life. The secret is to always keep my goals out there."

Good luck to you... and always remember the deep advantage of maintaining an "up" spirit. For sure! It will work wonders for you!.
Sales Management

Coping With <u>Fear</u>

Success in Selling and courage are inseparable. Without this characteristic few salespeople could succeed. The opposite side of the coin, which everyone shares, is fear. It is a natural instinct that acts as a warning signal against danger. Fear, as long as it is not excessive, is healthy. If it should become dominant, it can be overcome by understanding. The most effective remedy is direct action.

Two types of fear exist: physical and psychological.

When our imagination plays havoc with us, we often imagine all kinds of serious threats to ourselves. People, events and circumstances pose threats to our sense of well-being.

We are threatened when competitors take away customers because they are able to make a better offer... when a product we are handling is supplanted by a new and better item ... when we lose accounts because they move out of our areas... or if our suppliers change their sales plans and we are forced to make adjustments in our selling. Fear Is the end result of reverses of this nature.

Anxieties Plentiful

Financial difficulties, ill health, family conflicts, bad debts and bad news reports about national or local issues often lead to fear.

Our sense of security may be affected when new people enter the working environment. We might be threatened by the possibility of competition from the newcomer. A new manager, known for being tough, can cause anxious moments.

Studies of fear reveal three basic characteristics: ***they are common, natural tendencies of which no one need be ashamed.***
They are only bad when they prevent us from acting constructively.
They are sometimes confused with phobias as opposed to normal reactions.

Every normal person can expect to experience fear. To deal with fear, we should try to find it's cause. Sometimes there isn't any. What really happens is that we transfer an inner emotional concern to a convenient outside problem.

Many Remedies Available

Be of good cheer. There is a remedy. By trying harder and avoiding errors, we can get rid of anxiety and, once again, achieve successful selling results.

Fears are nature's way of warning us to be careful and to prepare for the task at hand. Look at fear as a blessing in disguise. By handling it correctly, it can be a definite benefit. By handling it objectively and positively, we can master it so that it will not have a negative effect on our ability to sell our products, goods and services.

Specific fears affect and concern all professional people. However, as a salesperson, you are unique. Few fields require as much daily assessment of performance or depends as heavily on one's ability to influence decision-makers. To a major extent, your physical and mental well-being are linked with your day-to-day performance.

Expect Some Failures

Success in selling requires ambition, ability and drive. It also requires the ability to endure failure. You can't expect to close every presentation you make. Learn to settle for an acceptable average. The failures and successes tend to balance each other, establishing an equilibrium that radiates steady progress.

The key to your selling success is to be optimistic on every call. A good way to look at life and your job as a salesman is based on the view that every day brings good and bad. Expect short-term failures in the same way you would expect good and bad hands at bridge and poker, good and bad days at fishing or good and bad days at golf.

The fear of rejection, many psychologists believe, is especially destructive for salespeople. Rejection often involves a lack of regard for sales people as individuals. In selling we often hear remarks such as "Many salesmen come in here, but I don't pay any attention to them." ... "I don't have time to waste on salespeople." ... I buy very little from the outside."

Wise salespeople never take curt or undiplomatic rejections personally. If they did, they would be undermining their own confidence. They also know that every buyer purchases from someone. If they didn't, there wouldn't be any business transacted.

Another major fear that confronts salespeople is the fear of making mistakes. Making a poor presentation or writing up orders incorrectly is commonplace. It happens to all of us. Don't let mistakes cloud your judgement. If you good-naturedly admit an error to a customer, it is likely that it will be understood and forgotten.

Another fear that confronts salespeople is the feeling of awe they sometimes experience when dealing with prominent individuals. Remember, they are no more and no less human than you. While they may be experts in their fields, you are an expert in your own area. You have a superior knowledge of your products, services, company and selling methods. No matter how important or glamorous your prospect may be, you are equals. If you remember this fact, your fears will disappear.

"Think" Success

Obviously, any normal, responsible person is concerned about the future. Nothing threatens or dampens the future more than chronic worry. It's impossible to accurately predict the future. We all make mistakes. The best we can do is try to perform successfully... and keep trying when things don't work out as well as we would like them to.

People who enjoy life have learned how to handle their fears. They don't carry a pack of worries on their backs. Instead, they radiate self-confidence. Their attitudes, in turn, inspire confidence in others... contributing to their success.

A cheerful frame of mind and a relaxed attitude banish fears. It's the best ammunition in your sales arsenal. Make it your goal to enjoy your work in selling. If you do, you will sell more and find it easier to reach your goals.

$Power$ Closing Secrets!

Classic Closers are available to all. The real secret is *how they're applied.* After all, the same words are available to the best-selling novelist and the postcard-scribbling vacationer. The way they employ these words makes a world of difference.

Closing is a little like swimming. Say you're swimming across a lake. You make a heroic effort but fail ten feet from the dock. Well, buddy, you've failed. So it is with closing sales. The close is everything.

Here are the basic closing keys:
1 The Beyond Any Doubt Key: You close by assuming the prospect is going to buy. Take it for granted that the answer is Yes! You are 100 percent certain, you can imagine no other outcome. This confidence is contagious.

2. The Little Question: By getting the buyer to buy something of secondary importance, you make the prospect tell you he or she is ready to buy. The buyer's name, for example, is the most charming sound in the world.

3. Do Something: Nine sales in ten Should be closed by physical action. Action is the easiest, surest, quickest way.

4. The Coming Event: You announce an impending event to hasten the decision. "Prices are going up next month. Initial this form now!")

5. The Third Party Endorsement: You tell stories about, or get referrals from, happy customers.

6. Something For Nothing: You end your presentation with a special bonus, appealing to the Something-for-nothing hot button in each human being. Many buyers, believing they are the center of the universe, will not sign unless they feel they're getting something special. This can be, and usually is, a trivial thing. But it often locks up the sale.

7. Ask And Get: At times, the best strategy is thinking boldly for the other. Use this carefully, at the right time, under the right conditions. If you don't ask, you don't get.

8. The Choice: Don't ask if, ask which. For example *"which formula do you want and in a 15 or 30 days term?"* In answering, your prospect is saying yes.

9. Appeal To The Pride: Paint a vivid picture in their head. *"Imagine how good it would be if* *you had this backpack with a power bank, with you all day long"* "*Imagine how you Will feel driving up in this new car!"* , *"Imagine seeing your skin glow everyday with this cream!"*

10.   Future Dating: Your prospect really isn't ready to buy now? Pin down delivery three months or even a year ahead. Better than letting a competitor walk away with it.

11 One More Thing: The prospect says no. You start to leave. Then you stop, inspired, and say: "Oh, I almost forgot to mention a very important fact. If you place your order this month, you'll get one case free. You simply can not afford to pass up savings like that, can you?"

12. Summarize The Plus Points:

Some prospects respond to a summary of all the plus points. They see an array of benefits marching toward them.

13. Pros And Cons: With some on-the-move analytical buyers, write out the pros and cons of your proposition, side by side. Naturally, you favour the pros.

But give a few cons, too. Whitewashing isn't credible.

14. The Logic Key: The buyer wants evidence. Give it in full measure. "It must be clear to a woman of reason that if such and such is the case, thus and so must be, as day follows night. Therefore, there's only one thing for us to decide… How soon do you want these books in your library? Will next Wednesday be soon enough?" When the buyer starts answering questions about delivery, she's going to buy.

15. The Intimate Close: One high-volume buyer says his most effective supplier whispers at the close, as if disclosing a valuable secret. "I leaned forward not wanting to say a word." The buyer related. I continued to follow. Before I knew it, he asked me to buy it. Before I knew it, I whispered yes!"

16. The Silent Close: One toiletries salesman doesn't say a dozen words. He merely shows merchandise. He points to this feature and that. He demonstrates. He lets the products speak for themselves.

Then he starts writing up the order and inquires: "How many?"

Or he takes out an order blank, marks an X on it, and says, "Here." It works! Silence can be powerful.

17. The What-If-Key: Don't say what you'll do. Ask "what if."

Mr james, what if I get the owner to pay for parking lot repairs, and go 50-50 on air conditioning? I don't know if I can, but if I can, would you accept that?

Most sales are closed with one of these classic keys. That's a science you can learn. Knowing when and how to use these keys… that's an art. The art of selection and presentation separates the upper 20 percent of the high earners from the lower 80 per cent in the thundering herd!

How To Set And Reach Your Goals

Mark works hard at selling. He makes his calls regularly, and he closes a percentage of them. Although he sets weekly, monthly, and yearly goals for himself, he never seems able to keep them.

Perhaps you are like mark. You have heard of the value of goal setting. Yet, though you set goals, you seldom reach them. Most sales training programs tell you to have definite goals, and you recognize the value of this advice. But what you really need is a practical method that will enable you to reach your goals.

In selling, the secret of success lies not in setting goals but in keeping them. To do this, you need more than goals. You need a system of record keeping that allows you to assess the factors that make success attainable.

Successful goalkeeping is really a marriage between the creative and the practical. Your creative imagination visualizes what you want to achieve. Your records should be your guide.

Establish Concrete Goals

For goals to be effective they must be concrete. For this reason, I suggest you write them down. This will make them much more definite in your mind.

Don't say, "I want to make more money this year." That is too open-ended. How much is more money? Is it more money than last year? Is it more money than your fellow salespeople? Would one dollar more be enough to meet this goal?

A better goal would be " I want to earn the sum of $20,000 in commissions this year." And once you set an annual goal, break it down into monthly, weekly and daily goals. For instance, if your goal is to make $20,000 in commissions next year, your monthly goal would be $1667. Your weekly goal would be about $416.75. And everyday you would need $83.35 to meet your goal. This could assume a two-week vacation and a five-day work week. If you work a longer or shorter week, you have to adjust these figures accordingly.

Call On Enough Prospects

When you have done this, you know what daily production you need to meet your goal. Knowing this, you must convert that number to earn the commissions you require.

This is where many salespeople get off track. They think in terms of their daily sales goals and the commission figure they need to reach their objectives. When they don't make the required amount one day, they go home depressed by the idea that their performance for the week has been ruined. However, by determining what each sales call is worth, it is possible to meet these goals... provided the required number of calls have been made. The law of averages generally works!

In order to find out what each sales call is worth, you must keep certain records. The manner in which you organize this information can be flexible. Some people use graphs. Others record their sales in tables.

The first thing you should record is the number of sales calls you make each day. A sales call means you actually talked to someone who had the authority to buy your product and you asked for the opportunity to give your presentation.

The second thing to record is the result of that sales call. If you work by appointment, record whether you made the appointment or not. If you sell on the spot, record whether you sold or not. When you close a sale, record your commission. If you work by appointment, keep a daily record of your appointments and the results they produce. A kept appointment is one in which you give your entire presentation to a qualified prospect. If the presentation was cut short, or you discover that the prospect doesn't have the authority to buy the product, it doesn't count as a real appointment.

Keep Adequate Records

Of course, you also want to record the results of a kept appointment. Did you sell, get turned down cold, or get a definite call-back? And if you sold, what was your commission?

After keeping these records for three or four weeks, you are ready to determine how much money each sales call is worth. This is simple if you have kept accurate records. Just total up the projected commissions from your records and divide the total by the number of calls you made.

Now you have a realistic guide to follow in meeting your goal. If you make seven calls a day and do your best on each call, the commissions will take care of themselves. This lets you relax when you hit a slump. All you have to do is keep making calls and the percentage will work for you.

Even after you determine your initial ratio, keep up your records. And periodically evaluate the effectiveness of your selling. As you improve, your dollar-value-per-call will increase. This means your future goals will be figured in terms of these new percentages. Yes, goal setting is great... but it is goal keeping that will guarantee your success in selling!

"Big Dreams - Big Results"

Ain't never met a really successful person who didn't have a bit of a dreamer in him or her. Actually, it's only successful people who know the technique of making big dreams come true.

Dream Spinning Sessions

The United Nations area was originally a real estate man's audacious dream. Laboriously and taking a big risk, he assembled options on all the properties in this run-down-neighborhood. He dreamed of the U. N. Building as a center for all nations. Then he proceeded to sell his dream to the late John D. Rockefeller, Jr. Who bought the land and offered it to the U. N. As an international headquarter's site.

This was just one of the many creative dreams of the late William Zeckendorf... "The biggest plans are the easiest plans to bring to pass."

Big Plans Lead To Big Results

When you project a big idea of necessity, you must put big faith into it, and big faith generates a dynamic all of its own. Moreover, to support a big idea, you have to give it all that you have got, and that, in itself, exerts a special extraordinary force.

People who come up with little uninspiring plans actually are matching minimal faith with little goals, and so it is not surprising that little comes of them. Big dreams, plus faith, plus big work efforts added to positive thinking-that is the formula by which big things are done.

Big dreams do not always make it quickly to big results, but for sure they go way ahead of small results.

Hunting For Prospects

We went out quail hunting yesterday, and spent the afternoon climbing up rocky hills and around sticker bushes and hiking down into ravines and through washes... and didn't get a darn thing!

And I thought it was a perfect quail country, too. Water, cover, food... What else does a quail need?

But they weren't there, and we got beaten.

It seems to me that perhaps we were looking in the wrong place - a spot where it appeared to be a good quail country quail would be, but the quail didn't agree.

Go Where The Prospects Are

In other words, we were "prospecting" in an area where there weren't any prospects. And it occurred to me that many salespeople do the same thing. We look for prospects where we want to look, rather than where the prospects are.

And often don't we carry this a step further and tend to talk to those people who want to talk to us, rather than to those people who need what we're selling?

Oh, it's much easier to talk to folks who like to hear our story, even though they aren't really prospects. And, let's face it; no one likes to be rejected, and to be turned down. So, it's only natural to seek out those men and women who will listen to our sales story, regardless of whether they want or need or can afford our products and or services.

Make Your Efforts Count

For example, if you're selling encyclopedias, you have to see prospects who have children and who can afford the cost of your set of books. Period. You may be able to generate ten appointments a day with older folks… but try aren't prospects, at least not good prospects. You might feel more comfortable working with men and women who don't have any extra cash, but they're not real prospects, either.

If you sell new cars, it's fun to visit with people who just bought a new automobile… but they're not prospects.

If you sell businessmen's insurance of some sort, you'd better be working all day long in those high-rise office buildings. You won't sell in the suburbs, although you might feel more comfortable there.

If you're working door-to-door selling a roof coating, you must talk to people who have roofs in need of repair... although people with good roofs will be easier to get appointments with. After all, they know they don't need what you're selling!

And why don't we prospect in the right areas? *Earl Nightingale* may have said it the best when he noted that, "we don't like to talk to people... about something they might not want to talk about."

Isn't that really the fundamental reason why many of us meet and see and approach people who aren't really qualified prospects? Because those people who really need what we're selling know they need it... and will be harder to "sell"

Find And Fill Real Needs

If you're in the air conditioning business, and want to stay in it , you need to see people who don't have a working air conditioning system... and you have to be where it's hot!

Just like if you're in the skincare business, you can be where the weather or sort, isn't really all favourable on the skin, you would know the best skin product or formulation that's good for them and make your presentation!

If you handle some sort of deck for installation around swimming pools, you'd best spend much of your time in affluent parts of town, where there are swimming pools.

While you may sell some of your line of jewelry or cosmetics to a man (perhaps as a present for his girl), your best prospects will be women; you should concentrate there.

In other words… if you run a cleaning service, you have to go where it's dirty. If you sell lawn and garden supplies, you have to talk to people with lawns and gardens. If you choose to sell firewood, your prospects should have fireplaces!

So before you head out tomorrow morning, before you start marketing digitally on your platforms and running ads, spend some time to determine who your prospects are. Remember, to be successful in selling, one of the things is to be a problem solver, is your product/ service solving a problem? Yes! It's always our default answer, because why shouldn't our products and services solve a problem? . Often, we waste hours on a hit-and-miss approach, as if we're operating on a random basis. Remember that the Hunter has to have a target before he can hit his mark. The same goes for all of us.

So, First figure out who your prospects may be... and then concentrate on seeing and contacting those people. Whether you like where your prospect may be doesn't matter. That's where you have to be. If you follow these little hunting rules, you will be a success in this game.

What To Do When They Say "*NO!*"

Have you ever examined your sales presentation in terms of the 'yes" answers versus the *"no"* answers? That may sound odd - we all want a resounding *yes* from every prospect - but the amazing thing is that all too many salespeople let their prospect get into the habit of saying *no* before they even ask them for a buying decision.

Oh, it's an easy thing to do, but if we can reverse the trend and get each prospect used to saying *yes* , we'll have a much better chance to get the order. The secret is to structure everything we say to lead to a positive response, not only for each individual question, but toward our ultimate goal: *to make a sale*

The process works like this: you examine your sales presentation to make sure that every question you ask a prospect lends itself to a *yes* answer. If you don't ask questions during your presentation, you're missing a powerful tool in your sales arsenal. If you do have an intelligent question come along in your presentation every few minutes, you're on the right track. It makes the prospect be in the moment with you, and feel really included and valuable, as he should feel. And simply, you need to adapt what you say now, to use this technique.

Find A Need

For example, let's say you're in the roofing business and have the universal problem-*no prospects*. You decide to take things into your own hands and drive around, in search of a roof that might need some work.

Most people don't worry about their roof until and unless it leaks, unless they have money and always want to look good. The roofs you will find don't leak, or their owners would have already called someone. Can you imagine a more difficult situation than to attempt to convince a homeowner to fix a roof that doesn't leak?

You probably also can guess the response you might get if you knock on their door and suggest a free quotation to *"repair their roof"*. No dice.

The answer here is to structure each question you ask to (1) get a *yes* response from the prospect, and (2) to lead them toward that final buying decision.

So when the prospect answers the door, you might want to say something along this line: "Hello, I'm blur Kooh. I'm in the roofing business and while I'm sure your roof doesn't leak, I happened to notice something I think might be of help to you. If you'll take a look from the front yard here. I'll show you what I mean."

You've been completely honest with the prospect - you haven't tried to hide your business or make them think you're 'taking a survey' or another of those well-used diversions. You haven't asked yourself into their home, either, so the prospect isn't too likely to feel that you might try to sell them what they don't think they need.

Describe Your Service

Chances are, they'll come outside with you. So haven't they said *yes* to your question? Good. This gives you the chance now to comment on how nice their neighbourhood is. It's also an opportunity to say something like, "over the years, I've seen too many expensive things ruined by plain water. And while a man's insurance will cover his things if his house burns down, it sometimes won't if his roof leaks and destroys them. I expect you've got valuable pictures or papers or something that's important to your family, don't you?"

Again, another chance to agree with you, and still they don't have to tell you exactly what 'valuable' things they have. Now you know what will happen if you tell the prospect they need a new roof. Or even suggest it: what you point out, with appropriate remarks, are any weak points that are visible from the yard. "See omg the edge of the peak," you might say, "how the shingles are wearing thin? See the darkness there? The gravel's worn and the paper's starting to show through. See what I mean?" You've made it easy for them to agree with you.

"See that soft spot over on the corner," you might say, "where the food dips down a little? Another place that might leak. See how weak that looks?"

Even with as difficult an assignment as mobile prospecting for roof repair, there are questions you can ask that will lead to a full presentation, to a sale.

Obviously, any questions you use will have to be geared toward a particular Problem you can point out, and matched to what you happen to sell. Someone who works on a door-to-door basis probably can find something to notice and talk to their prospect about, before they even ring the doorbell.

A furnace repairman might notice that a flue pipe is rusting through. A whimney man might see how the bricks are coming loose on the fireplace. Someone who does landscape work will notice soil erosion.

An auto repair service 'on wheels' might see some oil spots under a prospect's car, or a low tire, or a tilt to the car that could mean a problem. You can spot a problem in your field, can't you? Is your craft, you can!

Elicit Positive Responses

Whenever you're in front of a prospect, plan to ask questions that are easy for a prospect to say *yes* to. Here' are example phrases you can adapt to about anything you sell that are almost impossible to say *no* to:

"Would you object to looking at this?"

"Which part of this plan do you think would be of the most value to you and your family?"

"How many other ways do you think you might benefit from this?"

"Can you see how this fits into your total financial picture?"

"Haven't you felt you needed this for some time?"

"Can you imagine that you can actually buy exactly what you want at this price?"

"Don't you feel your family will be safer now?"

The whole concept is to ask leading questions that are difficult to answer with a negative response. Once you get a prospect to agree with you five or six times during your approach and again through your presentation, you'll find they almost automatically answer *yes* when you ask them to buy. Isn't that the whole idea?

Making "Clones" Work For You

... 8 ways to multiply yourself

Salespeople, generally speaking, tend to think in terms of personal selling. If they're going to get an order, they feel they have to do it themselves... personally!

It's possible, however, to "clone" yourself... to have silent helpers out in the field doing your sales job for you. If you're going to be successful in today's competitive climate, it's imperative that you start to think and act along these lines.

Veteran sales people take advantage of all the sales tools or aids available to "multiply their efforts." They get sales even though they're not physically present to do the actual selling.

Here are some of the ways you can multiply Yourself, and make your presence felt, without personally calling on each prospect or customer:

1.. The telephone probably is the most important sales tool of all. You can use it to make "cold calls" ... calling prospects listed in the yellow pages or individuals in specific areas to make appointments. Remember not to do all the talking. One major advantage of telephone selling is that you can ask questions and listen to determine whether you're talking to real prospects.

2. Direct mail is a multi-million industry that can work for you in many ways. You can use mailing pieces such as catalogs, brochures, flyers and sales letters to stir up business. You can fix these things up inside order packages to your customers, it makes you and your brand, as the case may be, to be with them and other people around them for a very long time, which is always rewarding. This is an inexpensive way to make another contact and multiply yourself without being present.

And for small businesses who wish to take their business digital, and even the ones already in the "era" it is more than a great idea to create an email subscription for your customers, whether you have a website or not, you can ask any prospects who makes an order to Subscribe to your email list for discounts, offer alerts, and other enticing specials there is, for your customers. You will find that it is a powerful tool, because once they like what you sell, whether you bring enticing specials or not, they will ask for another order, and that way, you're sure of continuous direct selling. No hard tack.

3. Advertising has been defined as salesmanship in print (or radio or television or social media). All sorts of advertising media are available today including newspapers, TV, radio, and an enormous variety of general and special Interest magazines. You can also use the telephone book yellow pages, direct mail, billboards, car cards, signs and other media.

Advertising rates often are less than you would expect. Check and learn what these rates are before you arbitrarily say, "I can't afford it."

Incidentally, don't overlook the local media opportunities such as programs for concerts and athletic events, high school publications and yearbooks. Interested local people read these publications and sometimes retain and refer to them over a period of years. All of which means that your advertising and sales "presence" can be felt much longer than you might expect.

4. Trade shows, conferences and meetings of all types are places where you can be seen by a number of people. Assuming you're in the right place, this is where you get "exposure" and where your efforts are multiplied. Instead of being able to see one or only a few people, you may get a chance to contact dozens or even hundreds at a time. Take advantage of these meetings to meet as many people as you can and to remind them of your products or services. Pick appropriate shows. For example, don't go to a farm show expecting to sell products for apartment dwellers.

5. Publicity can help you merchandise your products or service if it lends itself to the kind of news usually published. Most local newspapers will give you a write-up when you open a new store or launch an unusual endeavor at home. Some newspapers may even feature you in an article. Check with the local editor of the newspaper or the news station. Most editors and reporters are glad to tell you what types of news and information they are most likely to use.

6. Signs can be useful, too. You can use them to tell people where you are located or what kinds of services you provide. You may even have them on your car or panel truck. Some communities have regulations regarding the size or type of sign that's permitted. Check out the regulations if any. But look for opportunities to use them!

7. Giveaways are another form of advertising. Calendars, pencils and pens, appointment notebooks, paperweights and similar items can be purchased, sometimes at a very low cost, to advertise products and /or services. Don't over spend on these items but don't be stingy in distributing them either. And keep in mind that the selling process you initiate now is the one that pays communions three, six or twelve months from now when they will be just as welcome as they would be today.

Does multiplying your efforts, as described above, seem to take a lot of time and expense? You'll discover that it's a worthwhile Investment. Repetition and constant pounding on the mailbox and in the media ads is just as necessary as making personal sales calls. Some or all of these methods may work for you. When that happens, you have made it. You can be in many places at the same time…

closing sales and making money... all because you've succeeded in developing "clones" who work for you.

It's true that personal selling, face-to-face contact, is probably the most interesting and enjoyable type of selling. There's nothing like being there in person to make the sale and see the customer sign the order. But, unless you're selling very big ticket items and selling a lot of them, you have to multiply your efforts. By using the right techniques, you can be in more than one place at the same time... you can close more orders... and you can make more money!

And don't forget! *Use Good News To Create Letters That Sell!*

How To Increase Mail Order Results

Most mail order operators concentrate their attention on such considerations as the quality of the lists they are using, the effectiveness of the copy they have developed and product appeal. There are other factors which, while sometimes overlooked, can make a major difference in the results a mailing produces.

After you have satisfied yourself that you have the best possible lists, copy and products for your purposes, the following factors deserve a lot of your attention. In many cases, they can make the difference between the success or failure of your total effort.

.1. Sometimes, if not most, the exterior appearance of our packages are even more important that the offer inside. This is especially true when bulk mail is used. Bulk mail is much more likely to be discarded unopened than first class. To increase "openership" of bulk piece, select a "tickler" that fits the offer inside, but doesn't give it away.

For example, if pet care books are being sold, show a dog and cat on the package exterior. The printed return address (sender address/business address) also is a factor. Use your street address if an individual or unknown company's name is used.

2. Always aim for midweek delivery. Wednesday is the best day for a mail piece to arrive, whether at a residence, well-bill/shuttle stations/ carrier or business, either bulk or first class. Tuesday and Thursday are O.K., unless they fall right after or before a holiday or a three-day weekend. Monday, Friday and Saturday are poor. Fact right.

It's not always possible to time bulk mailings, or distant first class mailings, usually, however, a bulk mailer, working with the postal supervisor, can determine when a mailing brought in on a certain day will be delivered. First class delivery times are established from a map of delivery days available in every post office. Local next day delivery is achieved by mailing for early pick-up the preceding day.

3. Plan around the weight of the piece. Whether bulk or first class, there are weight cut-off points. If you go above them, the postage goes up to the next level. First class mailings that don't weigh more than an ounce cost 20 cents a letter. Suppose a piece weighs 85 ounces, but by switching to a lighter grade envelope, weight is cut to .625 ounces. Now there's room, weight-wise, for a second sales offer.

Great? Maybe. Additional offers in an envelope lower the response percentage of the primary offer. On the other hand, returns on additional offers may increase total profits. Therefore, present the additional offer in such a way that it's negative effect on the major offer is minimal. One way is to place it in a light-weight, 5¾ envelope, on which is printed something like "Another Great Deal Inside" or "For Your Secretary."

4. Work up a yearly mailing schedule. What are the "best months" for direct mail? January, February, March, October and November are best. August, April and May are in-between, and December, June and July are the poorest. Plan your mailing programs accordingly. Of course, you have to balance your mailings with the seasonal character of your offer.

5. Don't overlook the telephone as a supplementary sales tool in direct mail. Research in the magazine subscription sales field found that mail plus phone yields a higher response percentage than either medium alone. The home selling program of Webster, the dictionary publisher was and is a clever combination of attractive mail piece and telephone pitch.

8. Build Your Customer List And Analyze It for future applications. Much has been written about using customer lists for reorders, keeping addresses current, purging bad names and so on. This is an old hat. But how about analyzing the list for hidden trends and to discover feasible new product lines? For example, if there are several hundred "Edge Street" names, you might want to offer them a book describing the history of "whatever they are known for, or love most".

Have any of these ideas helped your thinking? Some may fit right into your mail operation, others may not work for you at all. But even the ones you can't use may help you think of other, still better ideas for improving the efficiency of your operation. This is what boosts response to your mailings and adds to your profits.

Win The Race For Success

In horse racing the categories are win, place and show. In direct selling, the categories run more to pace setters, pace keepers, and also-rans.

What is it that makes some people standouts in direct selling? Can the skills be isolated and learned? Increasingly, all varieties of professions and organizations are using comprehensive task analysis to identify the skills and competencies leading to success. Additionally, performance appraisals have moved from primarily subjective to predominantly objective criteria.

An immediate and significant advantage in moving beyond personalities and personal preferences in measuring performance has been the establishment, in writing, of specific job performance requirements. The benefit for those who choose to act upon the information has been two-fold:

1. **A clearer understanding of how leaders get to be leaders and**
2. **A step-by-step outline of required skills, in essence, a blueprint for success.**

Potential Application To Direct Selling;

1,. Efficiency Orientation: a concern with doing things better. This means reading Industry-related publications, setting aside time for professional renewal through workshops, and continuous review of operating methods.

2. Logical Thought: No matter how skilled the person or sophisticated the approach,

Selling always will be a numbers game: "X" number of calls = "X" number of sales. It's amazing how many otherwise effective salespeople fail to see the cause/effect link in this. The same principle holds in taking time to do an after-the-fact analysis of each call, asking yourself what worked and what didn't . In this way you identify what needs to be started, stopped or modified in your presentation.

3,. Productivity: Taking action before a problem develops or an opportunity is missed. This includes foreseeing or recognizing problems when they first appear, and making necessary adjustments so small problems don't become big ones

4. Self-Confidence: The ability to express confidence and be decisive. This does not mean being authoritarian, overly-aggressive, or a know-it-all. Genuine self-confidence comes with really knowing your product and being prepared to meet a prospect's authentic needs. It comes with experience and is one of the profits of trial-and-error practice.

5. Concept-Actualization: This involves actively thinking about new markets or new applications for products and services. In direct selling, it also means taking whatever works from wherever you learn it and finding a way to make it work in your business. Always apply concepts you learn.

6. Develop Others: Use performance feedback techniques to help others as well as yourself. Invite opportunities to stage one-on-one or small group presentation rehearsals and role plays. There's no room for stage frights in selling.

7. Concern With Impact: The ability to enjoy persuading and teaching others, coupled with strong personal aspirations. *Want to succeed*. Do more than us Needed for more survival… be determined to flourish!

8. Use Of Socialized And Unilateral Power: Develop your leadership ability. This involves building skills in delegating responsibility, in getting things done, and in creating a harmonious atmosphere. While socialized power has mostly to do with organizational goals and being a "team" member, unilateral power concerns you and your customer. The buying confidence you create in properly exercising socialized and unilateral power ultimately adds up to whether you have a customer :a one-time sale: or a client :repeat sales:

9. Managing Process: Understand what happens when you interact with clients. Selling is not automatic. It's more like stringing orientation, plus proactivity, plus diagnostic use of concepts, plus positive regard and so on.

10. Positive Regard: See your customers as people, not as potential "notches" on your sales belt. Cultivate an authentic service orientation before, during, and after the sale. Understand that you can fail without being a *failure*. The key is not simply what mistakes you make, but what you learn from them... and how you build success from there.

....your oral communication skill is very important in selling.

11. Self-Control: Successful selling involves self-discipline and consistency. It has to do with making good decisions about how to use your time and energy. It has to do with having the maturity to realize long-term goals may require sacrifice of short-term gratification.

12. Perceptual Objectivity: Refuse to be limited or shackled by subjectivity. Be a part of the interactive process which is the nature of all selling... as both participant and unbiased, objective observer. We can't learn from weak points we refuse to acknowledge.

13. Accurate Self-Assessment: Be willing to realistically assess strengths and weaknesses, to search out ways to capitalize on the strengths and overcome or eliminate the weaknesses.

14. Stamina And Adaptability: Physical energy can't be legislated, but it can be encouraged. Good eating habits, reasonable sleeping patterns, and disciplined working hours lead to an upward-spiral success pattern.

Rate yourself on a scale of 1-10, with 10 being strongest, for each of the fourteen competencies. 140 is tops. The closer you are to 140, the closer you are to the success you want in selling. Re-check yourself weekly. If you keep your tally in the 100+ zone, we'll see you in the winner's circle!

The Key To Mental Fitness

To be a success requires the health and stamina to work hard. And of course looking good is essential to making a positive impression.

But what about mental fitness? How many people budget time during the day to exercise their mental faculties so they're in peak shape to battle the competition?

I'm not talking about adult education courses, or reading good books, I'm talking about a mental discipline which can tone the mind the way regular exercise tones our bodies.

Most of us carry around an overworked and overburdened mind that bounces around from worrying about tomorrow's appointments to brooding over yesterday's missed opportunities. It's crammed with a jumble of impressions, fears, anxieties and concerns.

No wonder we find ourselves note mentally and emotionally tired than physically exhausted at the end of the day. No wonder we forget appointments and lose ideas no matter how many notes we make ourselves.

The solution is to put yourself on an easy mental exercise program in which you can discipline your mind so it concentrates on what you want it to do. Don't let it dwell on things that sap your strength and divert you from your goals.

Sweep out your mental closet, dumping attitudes and impressions you no longer want and fill it with the mental images and psychic calm you need to get ahead.

Here are some common approaches which can work for you.

.1. Repetition: The idea here is to end conflicting and disorderly thoughts by constantly repeating a single phrase. Pick a sentence which summarizes your most important goal and use it. It should neither be too general nor too specific.

2. Daydreaming: How many times have you had a job to do and your mind has wandered to swimming? Daydreaming is a waste of mental energy. It's like a construction worker doing push-ups during his lunch hour. Use this time to paint a realistic dream picture on which to concentrate. Picture yourself hearing the news that you've become a top salesman, or buying a new house after your promotion.

This mental picture keeps your mind focused on positive, worthwhile goals instead of wandering to unrealistic scenarios which just increase your frustration with your present situation.

Always Focus your mind on what you can do now. With such a picture before you, you'll see what you must do on a day-to-day basis to make your dreams come true.

.3. Relax: I know a lot of people scoff at meditation. It is, actually, a little more than mental relaxation. A tired brain can't be an engine for success. Learn to put your feet up mentally and stop all your thoughts. Go to a quiet spot, even if it's just two minutes in your backyard, and stare off into space.

Fix your eyes on a spot on the wall if you need to. If a thought pops into your head, don't try to force it out. Just let it drift past. Don't strain to empty your brain. Settle for slowing it down at first. If you get distracted, trace your way back following the rhythm of your breath, concentrate on each exhale and inhale.

After this, always put a positive and successful picture of you.

4. Physical Aids: Many of us ridicule religious idols and shrines because we've forgotten their true purpose. They are meant to focus the believer's attention on a higher purpose.

Look around your home, and workplace. What do the pictures and decorations do to you mentally? Do they help focus your mind on the objectives you've set for yourself? If they don't, remodel your surroundings. Instead of having a picture of yourself with your drinking buddies on the wall, hang a picture of yourself receiving an award. Or put up a poster of the next country you want to visit once you've hit your new sales quota.

Everywhere you look at work and at home there should be a little motivator pushing you onward and a little reminder of the goals you have set for yourself. Such aids help discipline your mind and keep it on the right track.

It only takes a little time to put these ideas into practice and they cost nothing. But in a short time you will find them transforming your mind from a clutter of befuddling thoughts into a powerhouse for success!

Helpful Links

Get in Touch: mscentguides.com

BONUS: there's a gift waiting for you once you Subscribe to this form!!

Get This Free E-book worth thousands of Dollars!

In case this link didn't work, visit the site above wait for a pop-up form! Add your email address and receive your free E-book!

www.ingramcontent.com/pod-product-compliance
Lightning Source LLC
Chambersburg PA
CBHW060844220526
45466CB00003B/1237